Combating Computer VIRUSES

By John M. Shea

Gareth Stevens
Publishing

Please visit our website, www.garethstevens.com. For a free color catalog of all our high-quality books, call toll free 1-800-542-2595 or fax 1-877-542-2596.

Library of Congress Cataloging-in-Publication Data

Shea, John M.
  Combating computer viruses / John M. Shea.
    p. cm. — (Cyberspace survival guide)
  Includes index.
  ISBN 978-1-4339-7213-3 (pbk.)
  ISBN 978-1-4339-7214-0 (6-pack)
  ISBN 978-1-4339-7212-6 (lib. bdg.)
  1. Computer viruses—Juvenile literature. 2. Firewalls (Computer security)—Juvenile literature. I. Title.
  QA76.76.C68S5325 2013
  005.8'4—dc23

                        2012008803

First Edition

Published in 2013 by
Gareth Stevens Publishing
111 East 14th Street, Suite 349
New York, NY 10003

Copyright © 2013 Gareth Stevens Publishing

Designer: Katelyn E. Reynolds
Editor: Therese M. Shea

Photo credits: Cover, p. 1 visionaryft/Shutterstock.com; cover, pp. 1, 3–24 (background) Gala/Shutterstock.com; cover, pp. 1, 3–24 (grunge banner; cursor graphics; search box graphic) Amgun/Shutterstock.com; pp. 4, 7, 8, 14, 20 (main image) iStockphoto/Thinkstock.com; p. 5 Comstock/Thinkstock.com; pp. 6, 27, 28 Hemera/Thinkstock.com; p. 10 Zeko1611/Wikipedia.com; p. 11 Rischgitz/Hulton Archive/Getty Images; p. 12 Alex De La Rosa/AFP/Getty Images; p. 13 Robyn Beck/AFP/Getty Images; p. 15 Jean-Philippe Ksiazek/AFP/Getty Images; p. 16 (screen image) David Paul Morris/Getty Images; p. 16 (main image) Ron Chapple Studios/Thinkstock.com; p. 18 Arcady/Shutterstock.com; p. 19 Joe Raedle/Getty Images; p. 20 (screen image) Ahunt/Wikipedia.com; p. 21 Mario Tama/Getty Images; p. 22 Bpedrozo/Wikipedia.com; p. 23 Garry Wade/The Image Bank/Getty Images; p. 25 Matthew Lloyd/Getty Images; p. 26 Yarygin/Shutterstock.com.

Printed in the United States of America

CPSIA compliance information: Batch #CS12GS: For further information contact Gareth Stevens, New York, New York at 1-800-542-2595.

CONTENTS

🔍 Words in the glossary appear in **bold** type the first time they are used in the text.

An Unseen ENEMY

Colin was impatient with his computer. It had been slow all week, and then it froze while he was working on his homework. As Colin restarted the computer, he thought back to when it first began to act strangely. It was around the time he **downloaded** a free game from an e-mail.

Suddenly, the computer beeped several times. An error message flashed on the screen. It said the computer couldn't read the **hard drive**. Colin's heart sank as he realized his music, photos, games, and homework were all gone. Colin had become a victim of a computer virus.

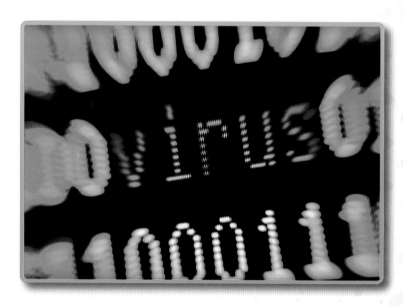

A Poetic Virus?

In 1982, one of the first viruses spread among personal computers. It was called Elk Cloner. It was a simple program that caused a computer to display a poem every 50th time it started. This virus was created by Richard Skrenta—a ninth grader!

We depend on computers every day for work, school, and play. A virus attack costs valuable time and money. It can result in the loss of one-of-a-kind files, too.

What Is a COMPUTER VIRUS?

A computer virus is a program that makes copies of itself. Just as viruses in people need a body to **replicate**, a computer virus needs a computer to make copies of itself. It often enters a computer by hiding in a program or file, such as a photograph.

Viruses are a kind of malware, a term that's short for "**malicious** software." Malware is unwanted programming placed on a person's computer without their permission or knowledge. Viruses are a serious form of malware because they have the ability to spread quickly from computer to computer, **damaging** hard drives.

MALWARE

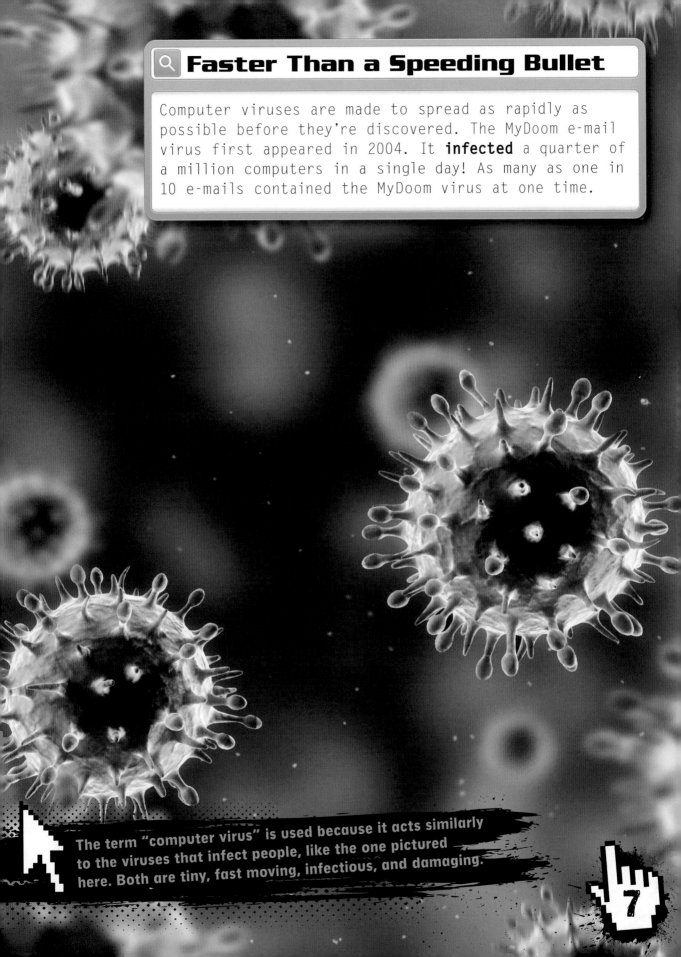

Faster Than a Speeding Bullet

Computer viruses are made to spread as rapidly as possible before they're discovered. The MyDoom e-mail virus first appeared in 2004. It **infected** a quarter of a million computers in a single day! As many as one in 10 e-mails contained the MyDoom virus at one time.

The term "computer virus" is used because it acts similarly to the viruses that infect people, like the one pictured here. Both are tiny, fast moving, infectious, and damaging.

Login

Password

Some viruses wait quietly on a computer and record **information** typed on a keyboard. Thieves can collect usernames, passwords, and credit card information this way.

8

Some viruses are made to commit crimes. This may include stealing victims' passwords or credit card numbers. Viruses may force someone's computer to send e-mails they didn't write.

Viruses can slow or shut down computers as well as the networks that connect computers. The Sapphire virus caused many computer networks to crash in 2003, including the 911 services of Seattle, Washington. Even so-called harmless viruses that show a silly message or picture, such as the Ping-Pong virus, slow down computers. It takes time and money to remove them. Viruses cost both businesses and families billions of dollars in damage each year.

It's Not Personal

Personal computers aren't the only machines harmed by malware. Viruses such as CommWarrior and Skulls attack some types of cell phones. The RavMonE virus infects certain kinds of MP3 players. Newer cars have computers inside them, making even cars open to attack.

Viruses, Trojans, AND WORMS, OH MY!

Viruses may differ in the ways they spread. E-mail viruses usually hide in e-mail attachments. **Macro** viruses hide in word processing and spreadsheet files. Scripts are small programs that make websites and e-mails look colorful and appealing. Web script viruses download themselves from certain websites.

A Trojan horse is another kind of malware. It's a dangerous program that masks itself as something innocent or fun, such as a free game or movie. Victims are tricked into downloading a Trojan horse. While this kind of malware doesn't replicate itself like a virus, it can still damage a computer.

the Beast Trojan horse

🔍 A Gift Horse

Greek myths tell of Troy, a city with strong walls to keep out enemies. During a war with Troy, the Greeks built a giant wooden horse and left it outside the city gates. The Trojans thought it was a gift and took it into their city—along with the Greeks hiding inside it!

It's very tempting to download a program that's free. But like the Trojan horse of Greek myths, a free gift isn't always safe!

The Love Bug

In 2000, over 50 million computers were infected with the ILOVEYOU worm. Infected computers sent e-mails with the subject "ILOVEYOU" to every address in victims' e-mail address books. People who received the e-mails opened the attachments because of the subject of the message, and their computers became infected.

Besides infecting other computers, the ILOVEYOU worm replaced many kinds of files on hard drives with copies of itself.

Unlike Trojan horses and viruses, a worm is a kind of malware that doesn't hide inside files. However, when a worm infects a network, it looks for other computers on that network to infect. The worm then copies itself onto the computer and continues to search for more uninfected computers.

It's common for worms to spread by e-mail attachments in order to infect many networks at once. However, a victim doesn't need to download any programs or open any e-mail attachments to become infected by worms. Just having a computer connected to a network, including the Internet, increases the risk of a worm infection.

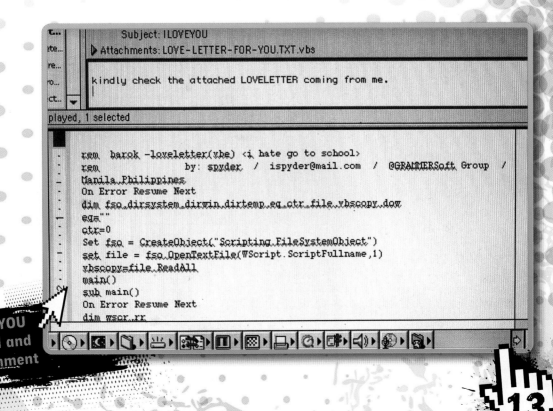

ILOVEYOU e-mail and attachment

E-mail VIRUSES

Before the widespread use of the Internet, viruses spread among computers through infected disks. Now, most computers become infected through e-mails. Infected computers use e-mail address books to send more copies of the virus. This allows a virus to spread very quickly to many computers at once.

Often, the e-mail virus arrives as an attachment in a program file. These files usually have names ending in .exe, .com, or .vbs. Viruses can also hide in .doc files, .xls files, and even .jpg photographs. Sometimes, e-mails contain links to harmful websites that download viruses to computers secretly.

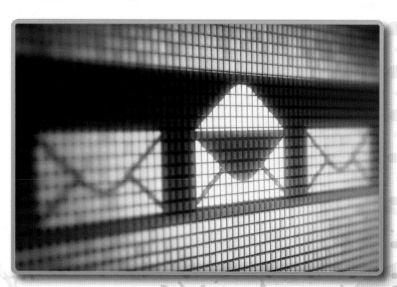

In 2007, many people received e-mails with the subject "230 Dead as Storm Batters Europe." When they clicked on a link in the e-mail for more information, they were taken to a website that downloaded the Storm virus to their computer. Millions of computers were infected with this sneaky virus.

People have many reasons for creating malware. Some want to be famous. Others just want to see if they can. Some people have gone to prison for writing viruses!

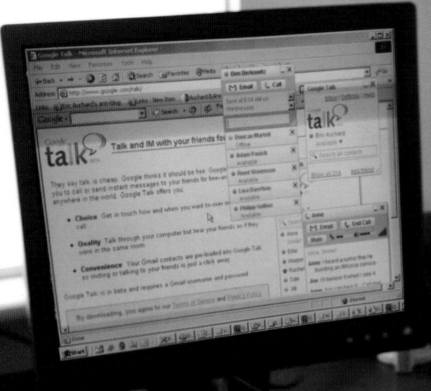

Because many viruses work by tricking users into opening attachments and clicking on links, it's always good to be careful while you're using the Internet.

Avoid opening e-mail attachments unless you're sure they're safe. An attachment sent from a friend's e-mail address doesn't mean it's virus-free. If you're unsure if an attachment is safe, call or e-mail the person who sent it to you.

Computers can become infected with malware just from opened e-mail, too. Internet **browsers** and e-mail readers run scripts that viruses can use to download copies of themselves. Users can turn off scripts in these programs, stopping the path for viruses. Users can also delete e-mails from unknown senders without even opening them.

🔍 Instant Messaging

Malware can also spread through instant messaging (IM). Just like in e-mail, viruses can be hidden in IM attachments and links. The same care should be taken with IMs as with e-mails. Don't open attachments or click links unless you're 100 percent certain they can be trusted.

Looking for Trouble: ANTIVIRUS SOFTWARE

Even without Internet access, viruses and other malware can infect computers. Electronics such as personal music players and tablets have been shipped directly from factories with viruses already on them. Viruses then copied themselves onto owners' computers when they were plugged in.

There are over 1 million different Trojan horses, worms, and viruses today, and that number continues to grow daily. Any kind of computer that interacts with another computer—including through e-mail and visits to websites—is at risk. Luckily, many antivirus programs are available to act as the first line of defense against an attack.

Time Bombs

Some malware waits for a certain time to attack. The Jerusalem virus erases a victim's computer files every Friday the 13th. The Code Red Worm tried to use infected computers to attack the White House's computers on July 19, 2001, at 8 p.m. However, it was unsuccessful.

Antivirus programs should be constantly scanning a computer, looking for viruses and suspicious malware behavior.

19

ClamTk Virus Scanner

File View Options Quarantine Help

Information   Scanning d79aa76ff6515a6d30e36e12d7582ff4.png...

File	Status
	Not scanned (size)
	Not scanned (size)
	Not scanned (size)
Ptimes Vol 3.PDF	Files number limit exceeded
Ptimes Vol 2 No 1.PDF	Files number limit exceeded
Ptimes Vol 1 No 1.PDF	
Chapter 07.pdf	Elapsed time: 25:37
FletchAir Catalog.pdf	

Viruses Found: 2

Status   Percent complete: 22
Files Scanned: 7930

In addition to checking a hard drive for viruses already present, many antivirus programs can also check downloads and e-mails.

Antivirus programs work in two ways. First, they search inside each file on a computer for known viruses and malware. Second, they **monitor** programs for suspicious activity, such as making copies or attempting to access the Internet secretly. If an antivirus program finds these behaviors, it will stop the suspicious program and alert the user.

For best results, an antivirus program should be running all the time. Then, it can catch viruses before they have a chance to copy themselves onto a hard drive. Antivirus programs must be updated often so they're ready for the latest threats.

Scan Result: **Virus *W32.Sircam.Worm@mm* found. File NOT cleaned.**

This file contains a computer worm, a program that spreads very quickly over the Internet to many computers and can delete files, steal sensitive information, or render your machine unusable.

This attachment has a virus that may infect your computer.
It cannot be cleaned.
We recommend that you DO NOT download this attachment.

antivirus program message

FIREWALLS

When a computer is connected to a network, including the Internet, the computer has access to all the information available on that network. However, the reverse is true as well. Anyone on the network can "see" and even change files on the computer.

A firewall is a program or system that acts as a barrier between a computer and the network. It monitors information moving into and out of the computer. It blocks suspicious information. A good firewall will allow some information in, such as websites and e-mails, but stop everything else. In this way, a computer is protected against dangerous Internet attacks, including network worms.

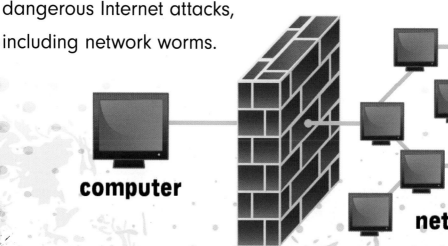

computer

firewall

network

One important way to prevent viruses from getting into a computer is to make sure a computer's operating system (OS) is up to date. Sometimes operating systems have weaknesses, called "backdoors," that allow others to control computers over the Internet. Updates are made to close these backdoors and stop attacks.

Talk to an adult to learn more about the firewalls installed at home or school. While firewalls may block some of the fun parts of the Internet, the prevention of dangerous attacks makes them worth it.

Prevention Is THE BEST MEDICINE

Unfortunately, the best antivirus program can't stop all viruses. New malware is being written every day. It can take weeks for antivirus programs to recognize and block these viruses. Still, with a little common sense, there are ways to keep our computers a bit safer.

Most viruses need to trick victims to click on a link, open an attachment, or download an unknown program. Always be suspicious of these things, even if they come from a friend. Do research online about websites, programs, and files to make sure no one else has found malware through them.

🔍 Ahoy, Matey!

One common source of viruses and other malware is **pirated** material, including music, movies, and software. Because these materials are often free, it's very tempting to download them. However, the amount of harm malware can cause isn't worth "free" pirated downloads.

24

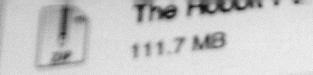

The Hobbit
111.7 MB

Illegal Download.Zip
111.7 MB

The Hurt Locker.Zip
111.7 MB

Pirate Music copy.mov
62.9 MB of 306.5 MB - about 16 minutes remaining

Pirate Music.mov
306.5 MB

Pirate Movie.MOV
66.8 MB

Malware creators will try anything to get people to download viruses, including asking them to visit websites where scripts can download viruses. If you think an offer is too good to be true, it probably is.

25

Have a BACKUP PLAN

Even with the best antivirus programs, the strictest firewall, and the most suspicious user, there's always a chance a computer will be infected with a virus or other malware. By making copies of important files, you can reduce the damage it can cause.

Backing up, or making copies of files, must be done ahead of time, before a computer is infected. Make sure copies of important files are stored on CDs or DVDs as these disks cannot be infected once they're made. Information storage devices such as external hard drives and flash drives are valuable. However, they can be infected with malware, too.

Administrator

Many people log on to their computers as **administrators**. This allows them to easily change their computer settings. However, this also means that viruses can secretly make changes, too. Logging in as a user prevents changes from being made without a password. This stops programs, especially viruses, from making dangerous changes.

PHOTOS

By backing up your files onto a DVD or CD, you make sure that one-of-a-kind files, such as photographs, will always be safe from a virus or malware attack.

While there are methods for removing malware from a computer, these may not always work. Viruses often hide in multiple files. If one copy remains, the virus will infect the computer again. Even if every copy is removed, files important to the operating system are often so damaged that the computer won't work properly.

Therefore, sometimes it's best to reformat the entire hard drive after a virus attack. Reformatting means reorganizing information, and it involves erasing files. By having clean copies of your important data, you can feel confident that your computer is once again virus-free and ready to work for you.

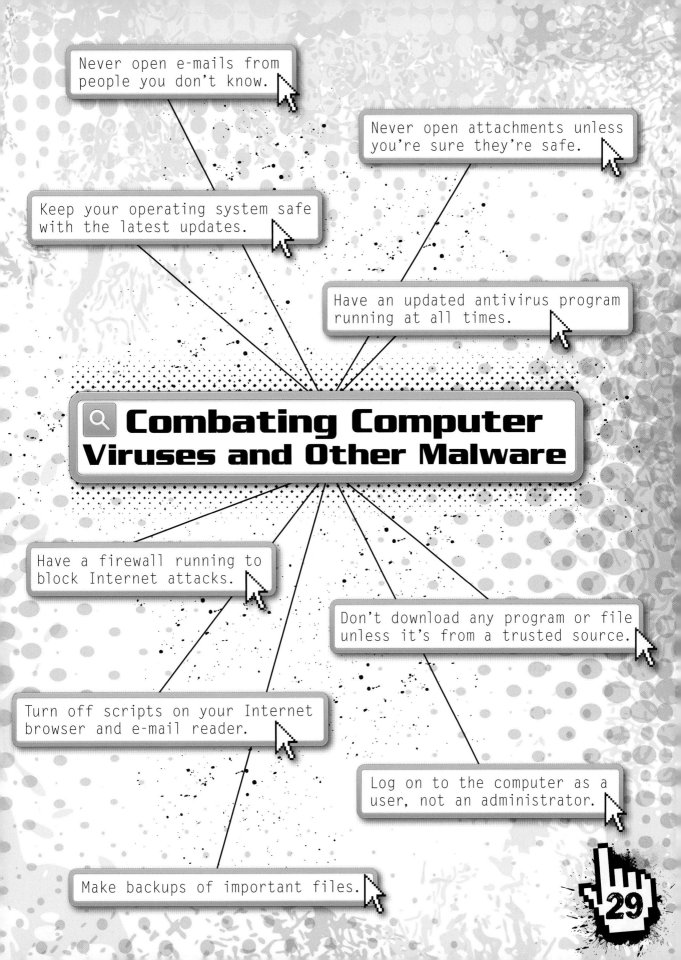

GLOSSARY

administrator: someone whose job is to oversee, control, or run a business, organization, or computer system

browser: a computer program that allows a user to get onto the Internet and look at information

damage: harm. Also, to cause harm.

download: to transfer or copy files from one computer to another, or from the Internet to a computer

hard drive: the part of a computer that stores all the information it needs to run, including the operating system, programs, and files

infect: to copy malware that can harm a computer's operations

information: knowledge or facts

macro: a single computer instruction that stands for a series of operations

malicious: trying to cause harm

monitor: to watch over something

pirated: illegally copied

replicate: to make an exact copy

subscription: an agreement to pay for and receive something over a period of time

For More INFORMATION

Books

Bodden, Valerie. *Using the Internet*. Mankato, MN: Creative Education, 2012.

Day-MacLeod, Deirdre. *Viruses and Spam*. New York, NY: Rosen Central, 2008.

Raatma, Lucia. *Safety on the Internet*. Chanhassen, MN: The Child's World, 2005.

Websites

How Computer Viruses Work
computer.howstuffworks.com/virus.htm
Learn more about many types of malware, and check out ways to defend against them.

Trojans & Viruses
www.childnet.com/sorted/trojansviruses.aspx
Read more about Trojan horses, viruses, and other online dangers.

Virus Information
home.mcafee.com/VirusInfo
Find out about the newest viruses threatening computers around the world.

INDEX